You Need
a Red Hat

How Sophisticated Ladies Free
Themselves from the Symptoms
of
YDD*
*Youth Deficit Disorder

By

Donald Huard, Ph.D.**

Piled Higher and Deeper

This book is a work of fiction. Places, events, and situations in this story are purely fictional. Any resemblance to actual persons, living or dead, is coincidental.

ISBN: 1-4033-6652-7 (e-book)
ISBN: 1-4033-6653-5 (Paperback)
ISBN: 1-4033-7639-5 (Dustjacket)

This book is printed on acid free paper.

e-mail: donderhead@Juno.com

1stBooks - rev. 05/20/03

About the Book

The red hat is worn by ladies over the age of fifty who feel an intense need to be e-womancipated, that is, to develop an independent "free swinging" lifestyle. This irrepressable urge very often follows decades of servitude and firm commitment to the well-being of unappreciative husbands and obnoxious children - often at the expense of mom's own personal identity.

The red hat symbolizes a grandma on the move, a grandma with friends, an auntie with a flair, a widow with a future. A sophisticated red-hat lady has confidence, class and a cultured sense of humor. These attributes help her to counteract the depressive influence of advancing age.

You Need a Red Hat offers a collection of humorous, thoughtful and incisive reflections about what it is really like to grow old. As you read the many interesting characterizations of "maturity" in this book, you will learn that as you age you are not alone if you find that your entire being feels like lead when you are supposed to be living the wonder of your "golden" years.

Why does it take you all night long just to get started doing what you used to enjoy doing all night long? Why do your aches and pains seem to be God's revenge for all of those good times you had, when you were too young to know that those were the good times? Why is it that when you give others the special benefit of your experience, nobody experiences any benefit?

This book provides a possible answer to those questions. It is entirely possible that, being over fifty, you may be in the early stages of the dreaded disease known as Youth Deficit Disorder.

The disease is depressing as well as progressive. Its insidious influence undermines confidence, erodes ego strength and sinks the aging female into slumbering resignation. It is a very sad process that must be counteracted by any aggressive means, including both chemical intervention and vigorous kicking of the feminine posterior.

As a symbol of reinvigorated spiritual and emotional identity, the red hat stands for restoration, recovery and rejuvenation. Those who wear it are proudly proclaiming their intention to enter a new realm of self-discovery and personal fulfillment.

Three cheers for the red hat! A powerful, very positive psychological stimulant. It can often serve as a supportive adjunct to any estrogen replacement therapy. Three cheers for the red hat, a form of ego enhancement therapy. Three cheers for the ultimate female Viagra!

The author wishes to acknowledge
the editorial assistance provided

by

Theresa Anne Huard

iv

Synopsis

Getting old ain't for sissies. In fact, it ain't for anyone, except for the fact that the alternative is even less appealing. Let's face it, it takes courage for us to look in the mirror and see the faces of our parents. It's disconcerting to feel as old as we are, especially after reaching the age of fifty.

In the sixties it gets even worse. It's called advancing age or "reaching maturity," whatever *that* is… Whatever it is, we don't like it. If that's advancing, then we would just as well back up a bit. We do not shine as brightly when we are old as we did (or think we did) when we were young.

In our seventies, we feel that we are beyond hope. Be not dismayed. Or, at least be a bit less dismayed. It can get even worse. Our middle gets bigger than either of our ends. Our friends begin to disappear as they go "forward" in active search of the Land of Eternal Consequence.

Is depression setting in? Are you beginning to feel useless? Maybe you are… Maybe, you ain't worth a tinker's damn.

You need a red hat. *That's* what will help you resist the disease known as YDD. Often referred to as "Pits"or "Dumps" disease, Youth Deficit Disorder can eat away at your nervous system and make you nervous, your emotional system and make you feel emotional and your attitudinal system, making you chronically bitchy.

Do you have YDD? Let's hope not. Do you see yourself on the pages of this book? Then fight back.

Go out and buy yourself a bright red hat.

To Margie

The sophisticated, red-hat

lady I love

Also by Donald Huard, Ph.D.

Behavioral Statistics: An Introduction
to the Basic Methods of Analysis
and Persuasion.
ISBN 0-8403-7408-9

Teen-agers: What will Cigarettes, Booze,
"Safe" Sex and Drugs Do for You?
ISBN 1-58500-314-X

Teen-agers: "Safe" Sex Isn't, But
Abstinence Is...
IBSN 0-9661606-2-2

Youth Deficit Disorder
ISBN 1-58820-543-6

Quotes for the Aged

"The older you are, the more important it is to take your sense of humor seriously."
Donald Huard, Ph.D.

"It takes all kinds to make up a world. Be glad you aren't one of them."
Donald Huard, Ph.D.

"Daddy used to say that when you are old it takes you all night long just to get started doing what you used to enjoy doing all night long."
Phillip McGraw, Ph.D.

"All of the great men are dead and you don't feel so good."
George Morris

"The shortest sentences are *I am* and *I do*. The longest one is *I am a mom*."
Margaret Huard
(the author's wife)

"Live every day like it will be your last. At least for one day, you'll be right."
Frank Sinatra

x

You Need

a Red Hat

if...

Donald Huard, Ph.D.

You need a red hat

if...

you want to be more than just a rib from Adam.

You need a red hat

if...

you clothed, fed, soothed and pampered your kids. Now **you** *want to be clothed, fed, soothed and pampered.*

Donald Huard, Ph.D.

You need a red hat

if...

Being safe depends
on your "Depends."

You need a red hat

if...

you keep getting food
caught between
your tooth.

Youth Deficit Disorder

YDD is also referred to
as "Dumps Disease."

From the Latin: "Dumpus ur Egoium."

Which is where you begin to feel that you are,
when you think you've fallen down into…

*   *

Life: Not the Same as Before

You're traveling less,
cause you're hurting more.
Your top is balding,
your bottom is sore.

You're short in the tooth,
got problems galore.
You're paying for youth
while God evens the score.

You need a red hat

if...

you worry about what people
think of you, when the truth is
that they rarely do.

You need a red hat

if...

The priest you call "Father" is twenty years younger than you.

You need a red hat

if...

both your spirit and your
income need boosting.

Emergi-Help

"Welcome.You have reached your friendly Emergicare Phone-Help Directory. Please select from our everchanging touch-tone help menu. Your panicky call may be monitored for customer satisfaction.

If your husband is beating you senseless,
press 1.
If you would like information on how
to proceed with self-administered
heart resuscitation, press 2.
If you are lying on the kitchen floor
with the dog licking your nose, press 3.
If your water just broke, press 4.
If your TV is broken, press 5.

In spite of your pain and lapses from consciousness, please be prepared to provide your representative with your social security number, dead mother's maiden name, your Medicare number, a Senior Supplement number, HMO identification number and the dog's given name. Please notify your PPO provider in advance of your request for service. Do not apply for service if you are uninsured or your doctor will not accept assignment.

You need a red hat

if...

you remember when
violence wasn't
random

and

marriage came
before babies.

Donald Huard, Ph.D.

Grandpa Never Listens

God consigns to a grandma the burdensome responsibility of making all of the machinery in the universe run along smoothly. She is the one who has to grease each of the gears, oil all of the joints and be sure to tighten every bolt and screw.

Grandma is inclined to worry and worry about all of these things. She worries that a tree might fall on the house, that a mouse might eat through the wiring and set the place on fire. She's afraid that the well and the cows will go dry. So, she has to spend much of her time trying to get grandpa to take her concerns seriously. But he never listens.

Don't you dare try to tell grandma that some things don't need her supervision, that is, unless you want your ears boxed. Grandma will tell you exactly what reality is…

Reality is that there's so much to do and that grandpa never listens. That's why grandma worries so much. She worries because there's so much for her to do to make the wheels run smoothly - and grandpa never listens.

You've got YDD and you need a red hat

if...

a full can of Ensure
is way too much.

Donald Huard, Ph.D.

Brain Dead

The doctor entered the waiting room of the hospital with shoulders stooped and with the appearance of a heavy heart. The message to the waiting family of the patient was one especially difficult to deliver. "I'm afraid that it doesn't look good. Your loved-one is in desperate need of a brain transplant."

"Oh, my God," replied the family members one by one. How could we possibly afford such an operation? We can imagine that it would be extremely expensive."

"Well, now," suggested the doctor, "if you insist on replacing his brain with another male brain the cost is quite prohibitive. But if you would consider a female brain, we could get one at a considerable reduction in cost."

"We don't understand," queried one member, "why would a female brain be so much less costly than a male brain?"

The doctor thought for a moment as the patient's family listened intently."Well, you see," *she* suggested, "female brains cost less because they have been used."

You need a red hat

if...

you're thinking of husband replacement therapy.

You need a red hat

if...

you lost your permanent teeth before you got your permanent head.

Leg - ality

Slowly old Uncle Ned maneuvered his wheel chair up to the front of the courtroom to face the judge. "Your honor, these people are the reason that I am in this chair," he protested.

As his story unfolded he told the judge of the bad leg that the doctors recommended that he have amputated. Reluctantly, he agreed to have the operation performed. However, somehow, the wrong leg was removed! So poor old Ned sued the doctor and the hospital after the bad leg was also removed.

A hush fell over the courtroom as the judge prepared to reveal his verdict. "Mr. Jones," he began, "I feel great concern for your plight, that of having lost your ability to walk as a result of your doctor's error. I can also understand why you feel that the hospital is to some extent responsible."

"Therefore, it is with great regret that I find myself in the position of having to inform you that from a purely legal point of view, you do not have a leg to stand on."

Donald Huard, Ph.D.

Septuagenaria 101

Some cards, a few thoughtful letters and a half dozen phone calls brought in the 70s for old Grandpa Don the other day. "You don't look seventy," said the nice lady at the grocery store. "You're only as old as you feel," said the thirtyish barber who unwittingly underscored much of the problem as far as gramps was concerned, what with the old man's aching back, labored breathing and his broadening girth.

Actually, it's not that bad. He doesn't feel any different today than he did in the last days of his 60s. That was just two weeks ago.

Grandma just turned sixty-five. You would think the world was coming to its end. "I look old, grey, ugly and wrinkled," she says, hoping that, for once, the old coot wouldn't agree with her self-assessment. "Now honey," gramps responded, "you don't look old and wrinkled. You just look mature. I really love that pretty face of yours. Besides, you earned every one of those old, ugly wrinkles by putting up with me for all of those years." Gramps was always very tactful. He needs to apply lots of finesse when he is living with grandma. He's, after all, not a clod.

The grandkids keep asking, "How does it feel to be seventy, grandpa?" "Well," he answers, "I guess I feel sort of, well, uh, kind of, uh, uh, accomplished. Yeah, that's it, *accomplished.*"

"You see," says grandpa, "the way I look at it is that I have two options. One is that I can be rather proud of the fact that I made it to this exhaulted time of life in spite of grandma and the other is that I can feel depressed by the fact that I have gotten so damned old. I prefer the first of these choices because that is the one that makes me feel accomplished.

Besides, there's a certain comfort in knowin' that if I check out soon, I won't be leavin' anyone in the lurch, 'cause now that I'm a septuagenarian, no one exects me to do much of anything except complain, eat and snooze."

Grandpa knows that he will be missed. But he suspects that the one the kids will really miss is grandma. She's the accomplished one.

You need a red hat

if...

you remember when,
whatever it was,
you just didn't
dare do it.

You need a red hat

if...

what you've accomplished is turning you on more than what you hope to do.

You need a red hat

if...

you need scissors to
take a pill

You need a red hat

if...

you're tired of helping your grown children "trash out" their playpens.

Donald Huard, Ph.D.

Sweeping in Seattle

Two brooms resided together in the same closet. It was inevitable - the man broom fell in love with the lady broom and asked for her handle in marriage.

What a wonderful wedding it was! The bride wore a beautiful white gown with a sweeping handle-length veil that descended to the floor and trailed behind as she approached the altar. The bride-broom stood tall, his golden whiskers trimmed neatly at the floor.

With handles entwined, they stood before the old priest and reverently recited their vows.

Later, at the reception, the bride whispered to her handsome bride-broom that she had a confession to make. "Honey," she demurred, "I should have told you this before. I was a red-hat lady long before I met you. Then, I was accountable to no one and I sought my pleasures wherever I could find them."

The bride-broom began to show signs of uneasiness. "What are you trying to tell me," he asked? "I've *swept* with others," she replied.

Bathroom Habits

Grandpa sleeps in his own little bedroom separate from grandma's so that she doesn't have to listen to his nightly snoring. He uses the littlest bathroom.

Grandma never ever complains about that bathroom being dirty. That's right, there has never been a time when grandma noted how dirty that bathroom was. Instead, grandma frequently describes the room as "FILTHY!!!" That's "EFF - EYEE - ELL - TEEE-AICHE - WHYYY - FILTHY!!!"

It's one of those techniques used by an older female to subjugate an aging, ego-enhanced male. It serves two important functions. One is to keep old grandpa in his place as an unwashed clod and the second is to give grandma the chance to show the old coot that her powers of observation and cleaning skills put those of her old man to shame.

No grandpa ever cleaned a bathroom to the perfect satisfaction of his spouse. Grandpa learned long ago that any attempt to do so was bound to result in criticism and failure.

You've got YDD and you need a red hat

if...

an exciting "all-nighter" means you sleep through without having to go to the bathroom.

You need a red hat

if...

you take your heavy glasses
off before checking
your weight.

Donald Huard, Ph.D.

You've got YDD and you need a red hat

if...

you pray that heaven
hath no anxiety.

Senior Flyer Discounts

"This is your captain speaking. Thank you so much, ladies, for choosing to fly with us on East-West Senior Service Airlines. We are always pleased to serve the ladies who wear the red hats. We hope that you have enjoyed your flight. We regret that it was necessary for us to replace the usual six-ounce bag of peanuts with a one-ounce packet of Froot-Loops. For your relaxing entertainment, we will show some on-board movies about plane crashes and sea rescues on your next flight.

This low-cost air transportation to your convention is made possible by using an aircraft with a remanufactured engine with a straightened propeller and boot-drag brakes. The pilot and co-pilot have been supplied with boots especially created by Michelin.

For your convenience when you arrive in Chicago, you may pick up your baggage in nearby Toledo.

Please unhook your seat belt before you leave the aircraft. If you are in need of a "pottie," please hold…"

You need a red hat

if...

you wonder why you are
punished for your
good deeds.

Red-hat ladies know that it's never too late.

The bride, white of hair, her footsteps,
uncertain, need guiding.
While down the church aisle, with a wan
toothless smile, the groom in a wheelchair
comes riding.

Who is this elderly couple thus wed?
Mature and patient, of them it is said.
Yet here they appear, grinning, near dead,
with thoughts of amore' in each other's head.

Who is this elderly couple thus wed,
with illusions of romance in marital bed?

It's a red-hat lady and him without hair.
You'd know if you had explored it,
that here is that rare, most conservative pair,
who waited till they could afford it.

Donald Huard, Ph.D.

You need a red hat

if...

you give them the benefit
of your experience, but
nobody experiences
any benefit.

You need a red hat

if...

you know your pains are God's
revenge for all of those good
times you had - when you
were too young to know
that those were the
good times.

Donald Huard, Ph.D.

You need a red hat

if...

all of your teeth are gone
but one - that aches
you good.

Swingin' 60s

It's not so much fun waking up one grim morning to the discovery that you have entered your 60s. As it says on grandpa's personalized license plate, you are just "2DM OLD."

During the 50s you still feel as if you are in the swing of things. After sixty, you have a problem just staying on the swing. You can't even remember when you were. On the swing, that is. Not that it matters.

You can't do with ease what you were able to do when you were in your 40s or 50s, like tossing a grandson into the air and catching him for a huge hug. You can't get the shopping carts separated at the grocery store. You're always looking at things through the wrong lenses.

Don't worry yourself about having to face being in your 60s. Be encouraged by the fact that it's a time of life that doesn't last very long. The 70s will go by even faster. A deficit of youth. Feeling unsure that you would want to live it again. Sure hope you've got a red hat...

You've got YDD and
you need a red hat

if...

you'll pay your grandkid a
dollar if he will find
a stick with only
one end.

You need a red hat

if...

you'd like a pause in
your menopause.

You've got YDD and you need a red hat

if...

you're wondering what
your kids will do
without you.

Grandpa's War

No red-hat lady would do anything that's this stupid. Grandpa got really put out with grandma the other day. Man, was he ever mad! Escaping, he got into his Jeep and proceeded to back it out of the garage. It wouldn't have been such a big problem if he had just remembered to trigger the remote door opener first.

By the time gramps got his Jeep stopped, the bolts, springs and track wheels were a' poppin' and whiz-in' around the garage so fast that the poor old guy thought he was back in Nam, duckin' the firepower of the Viet Cong.

Now, any damn fool knows that you're supposed to open a door before you go through it. But grandpa was so mad he just forgot the details. It doesn't matter what he got so mad about. Grandma was probably right to complain about what he did or didn't do. Grandmas usually are. That's what made it worse, the fact that he was so guilty.

She's not apt to let him forget about this one. What a blow to his ego! Red-Hat girls know enough to look for open doors.

You need a red hat

if...

*you have a decadent sex
life. You think about
it once every
decade.*

You need a red hat

if...

you find yourself too
soon oldt und too
late schmardt.

You've got YDD and you need a red hat

if...

people don't tell you you're beautiful, they just say "you're lookin' good."

Less Than Meets the Ear

Grandma and old grandpa have heard the same old stories from each other over and over for so many years. So, when grandpa says, "Did I ever tell you about the time..," grandma wants to run away, but she loves the old coot, so she just listens.

Grandpa won the war of Alaska all by himself. He told off his boss dozens of times. He often tells the politicians what's wrong with things and how simple it is to solve the pressing problems that they have a habit of complicating.

Grandma knows, of course, that there's less to his pronouncements than meets the ear. Still, she listens.

That's the way she gets along with grandpa. She backs him up when he's telling his tales to his old friends. Grandpa is real smart if he does his best to make grandma look special in front of hers. Each one is loyal to the other.

Eventually, one will miss the other. Much time will be spent remembering the stories— the ones that were less than meets the ear.

What Ith Obethity?

It'th the prithe you pay for
thriving at ec-thethiv feed.

*   *

Rushing Roulette

Then:

> Monopoly, dominoes,
> pick-up sticks.
> The games we played
> from eight to six.

Now:

> Different games.
> with different tricks.
> And if you lose,
> There's RU-486.

You've got YDD and you need a red hat

if...

you can't find
the other sleeve.

Why?

You wonder why your health
insurance payments must
be paid on time at 100%
when your benefits
are eventually
paid at
28%.

*   *

Terminal Shape

When you are gone
and no longer in peril,
they'll buy you a casket
that's shaped like a barrel.

You've got YDD and you need a red hat

if...

your shirts look better
tucked out.

You need a red hat

if...

you can't find your glasses
without your glasses.

You need a red hat

if...

you resent the fact that your
kids need someone to
blame besides them-
selves, and that the
someone is you.

Donald Huard, Ph.D.

Creaky Joints? Achey Bones? Bad Marriage?

ask your doctor about

Lethargozine*
Hydrozipizide Approximate

Specially formulated to cure everything that ails you.

Guaranteed to:

1. Lubricate immobile joints.
2. Grow heart arteries without surgery.
3. Restore frustrated libido.
4. Prevent senile pregnancy.

Frequently occurring side effects:

1. Immediate death.
2. Uncontrollable spastic gyrations.
3. "Out" continence.
4. A funny walk.

* This product not recommended for adults.

Pill-o-Talk

There's the brown one you use for blood
pressure
and the red one you use when you're sneezing.
There's the pink one that clears out your head
and another for when you are wheezing.

There's a white one for when you are aching
and a vitamin too big for the taking.
Then, when you conspire to put out your fire,
white powder for other than baking.

There's a mustard-colored pill for arthritis
and a tiny one just for heart-itis.
The relaxer for when you get nervous
and the green one that cures tendonitis.

A yellow pill helps with your weeping
and a blue one is helpful for sleeping.
If you're taking too much and the pills are a
crutch
then, your secret's best placed in safe keeping.

There's medication that treats all your ills
lessening your headaches, but increasing your
bills.
Whatever's your choice, there ain't nuthin'
woice
than facing old age without pills.

Donald Huard, Ph.D.

A Gamblin' Grandma

Grandma likes to go west with a friend or two for a little fun at a distant casino. What bugs her is when the place is so crowded that she has to stand in line to get a favorite machine. "Bad enough that I give my hard-earned money to those stupid machines," she says, "but standing in line to do it? I must be out of my mind."

While milling around in the crowd one day, grandma came upon Victor, who was playing and winning at three machines at the same time. "Won't you let me play one of those machines, instead of playing them all yourself," she asked?

Victor just ignored her, continuing to play as the others had to just stand and watch. He didn't care at all that others were waiting as he hogged all of the fun. It really bugged grandma. Frustrated, she told Victor that there was one of his nickels on the floor. As he leaned over to get it, she tapped the pay-out buttons on each of his machines. It took over an hour for Victor to get all of his pay-offs. During that time, he had to just sit there. All of his machines were inoperative.

You just don't get smart with a red-hat grandma…

*   *

Things That Would Have Made the First 50 Years Easier:

1. Curly hair if yours is straight.

2. Straighter hair if yours is too curly.

3. A six hour work day.

4. Returnable children.

5. A poly-unsaturated husband.

6. Every Wednesday off.

7. A bed-making machine.

8. A man who understands.

9. A child-washing machine.

10. A male household slave.

Signs that You Will Never See at the Casino
"Welcome to Unlucky's Casino"

1. "Over 262 million in losses in 2001."

2. "Drive-by money-drop box in front of the casino (you needn't bother to enter)."

3. "Instant debt machines available here."

4. "Over 250 money-grabbing slots."

5. "Lose your way down to zero coins."

6. "You can't lose if you don't play."

7. "Social Security checks taken from you here."

8. "Replacement shirts available in the gift shop."

9. "Come in your Cadillac - buses available to get you home."

10. "Support compulsive gambling."

Lost Love

Overwhelming personal grief is a most formidable adversary. Yet, its soul-tearing jagged edges wear smooth with the passage of time. We even learn to embrace our grief, knowing that richness of life is contingent upon the memory of both the pleasures *and* the pain. For, who would willingly forget the love lost?

*　　*

Renewal

Oh, to love again! And to be loved as well. But, is it worth the risk? What about the potential for more disappointment and anguish? For, true love requires commitment, the surrender of one's self to the needs of another.

"Never again will I let myself be so vulnerable," says one, offended by her past romantic delusions. "I will try again," says another. The first one looks back to the past to find a reason for avoiding future risk-taking. It is a self-defeating ploy. The other looks positively to the future.

Should you be satisfied with the calm and safety of the cove when unfamiliar waters offer the potential for enrichment? Thomas Aquinas once observed, "If the primary objective of a sea-captain were to preserve the security of his ship, he would keep it in port forever."

Donald Huard, Ph.D.

YDD at the Movies

You're showing signs of the dreaded Youth Deficit Disorder if you no longer like going to movies that feature death-defying helicopter crashes, exploding buildings and frightened maidens being chased by hatchet wielding psychopaths. You would rather be charmed by the characters you see on the screen instead of assaulted by their adolescent antics.

You think that sex should follow friendship instead of just replacing it. You feel that stimulation should be intellectual as well as physical. You feel that even the First Amendment should have its limits.

You're showing signs of Youth Deficit Disorder if you worry about the effects of exploitive film and music on today's children. As a grandparent, you feel a strong sense of responsibility to promote a nice wholesome emotional atmosphere, wherein the youth of today can develop respect for people of all ages and persuasions.

You are concerned about the youth of today. You are a grand red-hat lady.

Over Fifty and Groovin'

Arizona Red Hat
Ladies

Independence Day Parade
Prescott, Arizona 2002

Donald Huard, Ph.D.

Donald Huard, Ph.D.

Ladies
 with class!

Hey! That's
Margie in
the middle,
doin' her
thing.

You've got YDD and you need a red hat

if...

the only way you can beat
your grandson in the
ten-yard dash is by
starting on
"get set."

Donald Huard, Ph.D.

Too Much Ego...

Since grandma got that red hat, she's feeling free to express herself a bit more. She's quite fed up with men and she will tell you so. "The male of the species thinks too much of himself," she says. "Men are always fussin' bout how they look. After all, look at all of those glamour magazines that they buy."

Grandpa wears those underclothes that are padded just right to enhance his masculine figure and minimize his excess. Whenever they go out to shop at the mall together, grandpa always asks grandma if his hair looks alright in back and if his shirt and pants match. He always seems to need a perm.

Grandpa is very conscious of color, trying to get the right hue for his nails and eye-liner. He wouldn't think of wearing the same shirt the next day.

That's today's male- always worried about how he looks. "They's got too darn much ego," grandma says, *"that's* the problem with men."

You've got a red hat

if...

you want a necker's knob
for the steering wheel
of your red Mustang.

Donald Huard, Ph.D.

That's Music?

You've got YDD and you need a red hat if you hate being unable to tune the car radio. You can remember the days when you used to turn the dial to get your favorite radio station. Those were the days when you enjoyed music as you drove around to your favorite haunts. Now you are haunted by uncultured noise.

Those were the good days before digital. That was before video. It was when you tuned until you heard what you liked, not until you got the right number without being able to find anything likable.

Today you don't tune. You seek, search or scan. You run off the road as you squint your eyes at the numbers racing frantically past your station.

You miss your freeway exit. You're getting disgusted as your radio blares out the noise of strangled guitars, brutalized drums and raspy, sand-papered, smoked-out throats.

You wonder if you will ever again hear any sound that improves upon the silence.

You need a red hat

if...

you want to clobber
your daughter
upside the head.

Eternal Salvation

Jesus and the devil are accustomed to e-mailing one another to check their rosters for recently arriving residents.

"Is bad Johnny Goluzo down there with you," asks Jesus? "Yeah,"Satan replies,"he's the one who mistreated his wife and kids."

"I hear that Mary McCuttifield is up there with you, Jesus," queries the devil. "Oh, yes," Jesus replies. "She was a very fine red-hat lady. She deserves to be with God."

Suddenly, a bolt of lightening from far above shut down all computers. The devil complained, "Why me? I can't retrieve my files!"

Satan complained to God. "Why am I the one who can't find my rosters?"

Then a loud, booming voice descended from up in the heavens.

"JESUS SAVES."

Fascinatin' Rhythm

As a young Catholic couple planning a traditional marriage, Donald and Marie visited with the aging parish priest for their prenuptial counseling. Father McGilvey advised them to honor the guidance of the pope as regards to the problem of birth control.

"Practice the rhythm method," they were told, just as though it were a method that worked. "You can do anything you want in your marriage," the priest advised, "just so long as it doesn't involve birth control or having any fun."

For the first four years of their marriage the young couple practiced what had been preached. They had a son and two daughters during that time.

During the next year, the pair decided to take the Catholic way even more seriously. The method of control worked very well - for the church. It resulted in the birth of twin sons! They called the daughters the "Calendar Girls" and their sons the "Rhythm Boys."

Donald Huard, Ph.D.

Dominos Vobiscum

Dutifully Catholic, Viola hunted down her teen-age offspring in the afternoon of the last Saturday of every month. She was determined to get them to confession. How the kids hated being in that little prison cell with the aging priest who always smelled as though he had been eating cigars and onions!

Bless me, Father," they'd say, "for I have sinned."

On one of those Saturdays, Viola was running a little late. By the time she had rounded up the moaning herd it was nearing 5 o'clock. The angry teens complained all of the way to the church. Viola was weary as she approached the church door, only to find that it was locked!

"GOD DAMMIT!" she yelled, as the teens roared!

About that time, Father McGilvey came around the corner from the rear of the church. "Oh, Father," Viola said, trying hard to hide her embarrassment. "I just came to tell you my sins…"

"You just did, Viola," the priest responded, while making the sign of the cross over his throat with his eyes pointed toward the heavens.

"Dominos Vobiscum!"

*   *

Knowing

Perhaps in spirit at least, one need not be old to be a red-hat girl. Take, for example, the little first grader in the classroom who was drawing a picture of God.

"But no one knows what God looks like," her teacher proclaimed.

Without hesitation and without looking up from her work, the child responded, "Well, they will in a minute."

You've got YDD and you need a red hat

if...

you think more about where you've been than where you're going.

Grandparenting

There's no such thing as an aggressive, ugly grandchild. Some parents have kids that are downright homely, with big ears, crooked teeth and long skinny necks. Their behavior can be abominable. But, no grandkids are that way. They are all models of good appearance and exemplary behavior.

Parents, at the very least most of them, have children capable of expressing their mean-spirited self-serving, inclinations by chronically complaining and by pounding on their siblings. They refuse to eat what is served and very rarely pick up after themselves. Parents are driven to distraction by the aggressive rebellion in their kids.

By comparison, all of the grandchildren are beautiful. They tend to be polite, obedient and brilliant. Grandpa and grandma brag about them all of the time. If they come to visit, they are clean, quiet and considerate of one another.

Grandpa and grandma always assure their own children that they will be glad one day, when their kids are grown and having kids of *their* own. They'll say that it serves them right.

You need a red hat

if...

you've discovered that your chin has a clone.

You need a red hat

if...

*it takes all night long just
to start doing what you
used to enjoy doing
all night long.*

Donald Huard, Ph.D.

How Many Do We Need?

Grandma sent grandpa to the busy local WAL*MART to get some Q-tips. "And don't forget to pick up a box of toothpicks," she demanded. Since she got that damned red hat she's been ordering her spouse around like a drill sergeant.

Once in the store, Gramps searched and searched until he finally found the Q-tips. A package of 1250 was priced at $2.49. He immediately thought about finding another customer who needed some Q-tips, thinking that they could split the cost. The one light bulb that he needed cost $2.89 for a package of six.

"After all," he said to himself, "there's only ninety-eight years left in this century and half of these Q-tips would do us fine till then…"

When he got home, grandma wanted to know why he bought so many toothpicks. Being very clever, she noted how few teeth he has left. "Well," answered grandpa, "I wanted enough to build a miniature model of the Motel 6 - with a hundred units."

You need a red hat

if...

you wish men had to
suffer through
womanopause.

Donald Huard, Ph.D.

You need a red hat

if...

you want him to eat what
you cook - especially
if it's lethal.

Fatal Distraction

Old Grandpa Leonard had been feeling badly for the last month or so. He complained about his aching bones, stomach pains, poor hearing and a bunch of other infirmities. Finally, grandma took him off to see the family doctor who prodded and poked the old man for what seemed to be an endless time before saying that he couldn't find anything wrong.

Pulling grandma aside, he did offer a suggestion or two. "You take Lenny home," he said to grandma, "and give him active sex at least three times a day for the next month. And be sure you cook only his favorite meals during that time."

Grandma listened intently, thinking of how difficult it would be to meet the doctor's special requirements, especially since Lenny had been somewhat disinterested for the past few years.

When Lenny and grandma got back into the car for the trip home, the weary old man asked his loving wife, "Well, what did the doctor say?" "You're gonna' die," she replied.

*You know that God
doesn't want any lip
from you when
you get to heaven,*

*so she humbles you and
degrades you before
you make the trip.*

You need a red hat

if...

you're tired of doing
laundry for your
dirty old man.

You've got YDD and you need a red hat

if...

you're afraid to eat while you're on the road.

Why Not Now?

The day after you pass on to your eternal consequence, a large number of great new consumer products will appear on the market. The list will surely include:

1. real eggs without cholesterol.

2. a non-stick shopping cart.

3. car doors that respect little fingers.

4. a dog that meows.

5. a garden hose that can't kink.

6. anorexic ice cream.

7. shoes that don't pinch.

8. "fair" slot machines.

9. a leather belt that won't shrink.

10. quiet automobile commercials.

You need a red hat

if...

you wish you could tie
your shoes, then
slip them on.

You need a red hat

if...

*your nickels fall through
the quarter machines.*

Things That Give Comfort to Oldsters

1. "Thank you" notes.

2. Pictures of the grandkids.

3. Buffi sleeping within petting range.

4. Enduring red-hat friends.

5. Their own bathroom.

6. A new jar of Marmalade.

7. Respect for tools.

8. Letters *to* home.

9. Seeing their children struggling with *their* children.

10. A "thank you" for doing the laundry.

You need a red hat

if...

the cord keeps coming out of
the top of the phone and
people don't talk
loud enough.

Donald Huard, Ph.D.

Pitpom

Buffi weighs in at just under nine pounds. He's a scrappy little pomeranian who thinks that anything moving within his range is a threat. He's so fiercely protective of grandma and grandpa that he even protects them from each other. If grandma is in grandpa's office, he gets upset. If grandpa gets too friendly with grandma, Buffi gets upset. Hugging is out, that is, if Buffi is in the room. It's not that he's jealous, you should understand, he just knows that some things ain't right.

If either of his "parents" leaves the house for awhile, Buffi takes his rage out on his poor teddy by mercilessly shaking the stuffins' out of it. In the evening, Buffi can be found either on grandma's lap or next to grandpa on his recliner chair. He's smart enough to spend about equal time in each place so's not to offend anyone or show any favoritism.

Grandpa calls him a pest, but when Buffi goes to the land of canine consequence, he'll be sorely missed and grandma and grandpa will be without the badly needed protection afforded them by their ferocious, loving, nine-pound pitpom.

You need a red hat

if...

marriage means separate
bedrooms.

You've got YDD

if...

you have a choice - pay for your prescriptions or eat.

Older Siblings

Even when you've become old, you're fortunate if you have an older brother or a big sister to love and admire. You find yourself remembering back to the old days when your brother let you borrow his skis or when he gave you a few bucks to cover the cost of an evening when you had a special date.

"Big" sister was the one who comforted you when your special sweetheart, the one who was going to be your everlasting love, decided to comfort someone else. Your sister tried to teach you about the ways of women, when there was no way in hell that you could understand any of what she was saying.

Big brother and "sis" did their best to keep you calm when dad and mom got into their fightin' moods. Guess, 'cause they were older, they knew that mom and dad loved each other and that they just had to slug it out now and then.

Big brothers and "big" sisters. The older you get, the more you wish you could keep them forever.

You've got YDD and you need a red hat

if...

your chair needs new brakes.

The Naked Truth

Grandpa really doesn't care whether he wears his beard or not. Really, he only grew one to please grandma because she thought he looked a little better with one than without - something about looking better if you hide more of what you look like. Of course, grandma didn't say it that way.

Grandma says that most people look a bit better with their clothes on than they do naked. Now, grandpa might argue with that just a bit, especially when he's lookin' at the ladies on *Hot-stuff* TV.

The problem comes when grandma tells him that his beard is too long, so he goes to the barber. Then she complains that he got it cut too short. Or that it was cut wrong. Grandma's an expert on how it should be cut, but not on cuttin' it. His beard is always way too long, too short, too crooked, too grey or too shabby.

Grandpa solved the problem once - shaved his old chin as bald as a baby's bee-hind. Grandma nearly died! She likes him better when he is fully covered.

You've got YDD and you need a red hat

if...

you're afraid to increase
your heart rate to
over forty.

You've got YDD

if...

your fridge is littered with half-filled Coke cans.

You need a red hat

if...

your other hats
aren't working.

The Senile Razzberry

Grandpa wants an "Aooogah" horn for his Jeep for Christmas. He hasn't told grandma yet, 'cause if he does, she'll say he's got loose timbers in his rafters.

Grandpa is tired of all of those mean city yuppies who keep honking him out of the way on the freeways. He's too nice to yell out of the window like the young folks do, but he sure could have fun sassin' at them in the old-fashioned way.

As for grandma, he's been thinking of getting her something that might improve her kitchen skills, like one of those new fangled ovens that flushes.

Well, what will grandma think about all of this? Actually, she wouldn't care less. She's got a red hat now and she's off playing at the mall.

The young guys keep coming up to ask the girls what the red hats are for. And the "red-hat" girls are enjoying every minute of it.

"Do your thing, grandpa..."

You need a red hat

if...

you know that good things
come from God, but
bad things just
happen.

You've got YDD

if...

you wish you knew now
what you thought
you knew then.

You've got YDD

if...

*you wish you didn't know
now what you didn't
know then.*

You've got YDD

if...

There's an extra button
at the bottom.

Donald Huard, Ph.D.

Belly Achin'

Grandpa really ought to do something about that rounded belly of his. Grandma keeps sneakin' up on him to pull his shirt loose in front so's the spread doesn't show so much. She likes the old man to look nice, don'tcha know, not like he really is.

It doesn't help. There that belly is, for all the world to see. Grandpa isn't that concerned. After all, seventy years of workin' ought to mean that he has proved his worth - and his girth, be it appreciated or not. Besides, it's *his* belly. And grandma's doin' some saggin' herself these days. Of course, if he were to mention it, he'd be sleeping in the garage.

Grandpa's belt used to be level around his waist. Now it's level only in the back. Then it goes around his left hip, drops under his middle across the front then goes back up to cross over his right hip. Its configuration resembles that of the serpentine belt on his Cherokee Jeep. It drives the water pump.

Grandma needs a red hat. Grandpa needs red suspenders—so's he won't embarrass grandma.

Knowin' Where You Is...

Grandma really gets annoyed when she and grandpa are traveling and the old coot won't admit it when he gets lost. Usually, they are on the way to visit the grandkids and gramps makes a wrong turn. "Why don't you watch where you're going," she asks? Then comes the denial. "We aren't lost, we're just taking a shortcut."

The old man has developed a few clever ways to discourage anyone from asking where the hell they are or which way they should go to get to the kids.

Examples: "It ain't no use lookin' for where we is, 'cause we ain't got there yet." And, "You just can't get there from here. First you gotta go over there, then you can get there from there. But we gotta hurry. No time for little unnecessary stops, like goin' to the pottie. Go when you get there," he says.

"Besides, it might start snowing. Then where will we be? We ain't got chains except for the one lockin' on the propane tank, but it's empty anyhow."

101

Donald Huard, Ph.D.

Grandpa Wonders...

Grandpa Don has grown content with the fact that he doesn't know a lot of things. Some people have to have an answer for just about everything. But, grandpa knows there are some things he's never going to figure out, like tryin' to outsmart grandma.

Some things do confuse grandpa. He's never going to figure out how a clock can wind down without time going slower, or why, as *he* winds down, time goes faster.

He has always wondered how and where marshmallows are grown. He says he really doesn't need to know what heaven is. And that if all goes well, he won't need to find out about hell. He's been happy with his life - with the women and children who have challenged his days and enriched his many years.

Grandpa regrets not looking the way he did when he was young, say, in his fifties. He often looks in the mirror and asks himself, "Why did it have to take so damned long to get this good looking?"

You need a red hat

if...

*you drink soda that's
used for baking.*

Donald Huard, Ph.D.

You've got YDD and you need a red hat

if...

you'll vote for Satan if you
know he will increase
your old age
benefits.

You need a red hat

if...

instead of wanting more,
you just want to keep
what you have.

You need a red hat

if...

you would like to give back one of your "babies."

You need a red hat

if...

you'd like your old man
to experience childbirth.

Donald Huard, Ph.D.

You need a red hat

if...

you're so mad at your man that
you
want to sic Dr. Phil on him.

Gifted

No parent has lived a life more advantaged than the one who has shared it with a loving daughter. From the very beginning of her life, a daughter inspires her mother. She gives her father the benefit of her treasured charm.

From teddy bears to braces, to prom and motherhood, a loving daughter enriches the lives of all. Mom and dad enjoy the memory of her spirited childhood. They thrive on their observations of her accomplishments as an adult and lean on daughter for her abundant, endearing support during their declining years.

A daughter's responsibility toward her parents does have limits, however. Endearing support can easily transcend into possessive entrapment by the aged.

A daughter's loving concern for her parents should be balanced well with the need for progression toward her very own personal objectives. Nothing should interfere with the quest for the sophisticated lady to enjoy her e-womancipation. She should live with the knowledge that *she* is important - that *she* is entitled to her own life of personal fulfillment.

You need a red hat

if...

you need a nap
after your breakfast.

You need a red hat

if...

you would rather feed steak
to your dog than to
your husband.

Donald Huard, Ph.D.

Pullin' Her Leg

Grandpa had the old devil in his eye when he told grandma about the lady who was flirtin' with him in the grocery store. "Why, that lady followed me around like a love-sick teen-ager," he teased. He always did enjoy getting a rise out of grandma.

"And she was a real looker, too. Then she got in line in front of me to check out and kept smiling at me. She was gone before I realized that she had told the clerk that she was with me and that *I* was going to pay the bill!"

Gramps got very serious. "When I realized what she did, I chased that lady out to the parking lot and saw her loadin' her station wagon in a hurry, tryin' to get away. She started kickin' at me when I tried to stop her. Then this big motorcycle-lookin' guy is askin' her if she needs help. I got hold of her leg."

Grandma asked, "Well, for God's sake, what did you do?"

"Oh, I just kept pullin' her leg, grandma," the old man chuckled, "the same way *I* is pullin' *yours*."

You've got YDD and you need a red hat

if...

your colleagues all look
older than you, but
they aren't.

You need a red hat

if...

your circumference is the same as your height.

Serenity

Grandma and grandpa are old now. They share concern about how their grown children are handling *their* parental responsibilities during today's troubled times. But then, grandma and grandpa wonder if children were ever raised during times that were *un*troubled? The new parents need grandparent support from time to time, tempered with wisdom and understanding.

Grandma and grandpa have been there - done that! Now they get to enjoy the visits of the grandkids, followed by the relief of seeing the rear tail lights of the family's SUV disappearing into the sunset at the end of a busy day.

For the oldsters it's back to the serenity of their little nest in the pines. The dog quiets down. Then grandma tunes the T V to the Wheel of Fortune. Grandpa settles into his newspaper. Soon he is enjoying a relaxing snooze.

Grandma sews on a little child's dress. Her dear heart is filled with love and concern for her childrens' children. God keep them safe.

You've got YDD and you need a red hat

if...

you plan fewer miles between potty stops.

You need a red hat

if...

you look in the mirror and wonder why it took so little time to get so ugly.

You've _got_ a red hat

_if..._

you look in the mirror and
wonder why it took so
long to get this
good looking.

You've got a red hat

if...

you don't mind waiting
for the glue to dry
because
you believe that all is
well that mends
well.

Donald Huard, Ph.D.

Epilogue

So there… Now you know what being a red-hat girl is all about. You've committed yourself to determined resistance. You just aren't going to give in to the devastating, sad effects of Youth Deficit Disorder. After all, who needs it? Life is too short to live it with your bottom draggin' in the sand.

Being a red-hat girl means that for the first time in a lot of years, you're going to do some neat things for *yourself.* And the best part of it is that you aren't going to feel the slightest bit guilty.

You've earned a little independence and you're going to have a very long-lasting fling.

So look out world, here comes

the sophisticated lady,

the one who loves purple and wears a big bright

Red Hat.

Donald Huard, Ph.D.

About the Author

Donald Huard spent his entire life taking too much of it too seriously. Now, as a septuagenarian, he looks back on his fifties and sixties and wonders why he didn't take more time out to have more fun.

He admires the ladies who wear bright red hats, those women over the age of fifty who are dedicated to the enjoyment of well-deserved, e-womancipated self-indulgence.

Life is much too short and too precious to live it overwhelmed by youth deficit-induced depression. The author applauds the red-hat ladies who are eager to enjoy life to the fullest.

Emeritus professor of psychology at Phoenix College, Dr. Huard and his wife Margaret now thrive as retirees in the mountains near Prescott, Arizona.

www.ingramcontent.com/pod-product-compliance
Lightning Source LLC
Chambersburg PA
CBHW051425280526
45785CB00003B/1160